What This Book Will Do for You

By the time you finish reading this book, you'll be able to live up to the terms of a psychological contract that exists between you and the people who work for you. You'll be able to clarify roles and expectations, use appropriate, nonmanipulative rewards as positive reinforcers, and apply effective negative reinforcement for taking corrective action when performance or conduct does not meet expectations. In short, you'll learn what it takes to be an encourager rather than a boss.

Other Titles in the Successful Office Skills Series

HOW TO GET THE

BEST

OUT OF

PEOPLE

Donald H. Weiss

amacom
American Management Association

Library of Congress Cataloging-in-Publication Data

Weiss, Donald H., 1936–
    How to get the best out of people.
    (The Successful office skills series)
    Includes index.
    1. Employee motivation.   2. Incentives in industry.
I. Title. II. Series.
HF55495.M63W43   1988   658.3'14   88-4769
ISBN 0-8144-7701-1

Printing number

10 9 8 7 6 5 4 3 2 1

CONTENTS

Introduction

Being an Encourager Instead of a Boss

Not to have to *do* anything! To do nothing at all! Isn't that everyone's ultimate fantasy? Probably not.

People aren't built that way. Most welfare recipients want to do something with their lives. People with the means for doing nothing prefer activity to apathy. And when people come to work for you, they come motivated, committed to doing their very best. The motivation to work comes from within a person, and your job as supervisor is to create a productive environment and encourage his or her commitment.

Now you can read all about motivation theories, understanding them inside and out, but *applying* them—that's a different story altogether! Understanding tells you *why* you should supply incentives and what kinds of incentives *might* meet basic human needs. Application tells you *how* to function in the real world. So, in this book, you'll read only a bit about theories of motivation, but mostly you'll read about practical how-to's.

In the end, you'll be better able to live up to terms of the psychological contract between you and your employees. You'll be able to clarify roles and expectations, use appropriate, nonmanipulative rewards as positive reinforcers, and use effective negative reinforcement for taking corrective action when performance or conduct doesn't meet expectations. In short, you'll learn what it takes to be an encourager instead of a boss.

Chapter 1

Is It Really Possible to Motivate Others?

People expect supervisors to be, among other things, "motivators." Now that's not as simple as it may seem, not only because the material with which you have to work may not be amenable to motivating but because it could be that motivating other people is not even possible.

A minidebate rages in the self-development book world: Can you or can you not motivate anyone other than yourself? Management consultants usually take one side (motivation comes from within the individual), motivational speakers and writers take the other (you can motivate someone else). Well, can you or can't you?

Yes. This book takes both sides, because the argument is a semantic straw man that hinges on the *definitions* of the words "motivation" and "motivator."

If you define "motivation" as the energy or drive that mobilizes a person's resources toward achieving a goal, motivation comes from within. Synonyms include "urge," "itch," "yen," "desire," "wish," "want," "driver," "spur," and "demand." In this sense, only you are responsible for your own motivation—for what drives you.

If you define "motivator" as a person who influences other people, helps them reach a goal, provides incentives for success, creates a positive, productive environment in which goals can be achieved, you can be a motivator. Synonyms include "encourager," "persuader," "influencer," "goad," "arouser," "stimulator." In this sense, almost anyone can be a motivator.

Motivating Other People

Creating an environment in which people can feel good about you, themselves, and each other and feel confident that they can meet their own needs while making a contribution to the group.

Motivating includes *cheerleading* (exhorting, psyching up), but often cheerleaders turn off more people than they turn on. Moreover, the cheers have only a short-term effect. I take the position that instead of cheerleading, positive, supportive behavior and reasonable enthusiasm characterize an effective motivator.

From these definitions, it follows that you can motivate people for good or for evil—draw out the best or the worst from them. John Kennedy motivated; so did Adolf Hitler. But most people agree that Kennedy drew out the best from many Americans, leading them in their pursuit of life, liberty, and happiness, while Hitler drew out the worst from many Germans, leading them to acts of unbelievable barbarism.

The "readiness factor" refers to a person's vulnerability or openness to new or different ideas, to stimuli that tap into unrecognized motives or ways of satisfying needs or feelings. Without the readiness factor, how else could a Jim Jones persuade hundreds of people to kill themselves by mass suicide?

If people aren't motivated to do something or to achieve a goal, you may be able to persuade them to do things they would rather not do, but unless they are ready to assume the motivator's attitudes and values, the behavior won't be permanent. The readiness factor isn't there.

A person has to be ready to give in, or nothing you can do will budge him or her to follow your lead, because the person's *motivated to do something else.* In Chapter 6, you'll see the importance of knowing what drives your employees and what they're ready (or willing) to accept.

A metaphor from the *Star Wars* movies summarizes the entire issue: "The Force" is *with* Luke Skywalker. All Obi Wan Kenobi and Yoda can do is help the young man discover The Force within himself. These characters are motivators in the sense used in this book.

The Emperor fails as a motivator because he demands total control over The Force within Luke. Whereas Ben and Yoda are encouragers, the Emperor is *the boss*. You, too, have to decide which of the two you will be.

Creating a Productive Environment

The sidebar on page 3 discusses motivating others by creating a productive environment. The answer to "How do you do that?" consists of some pretty basic but not always easy-to-implement ideas:

- Expect the best to get the best; set high standards and expect people, including yourself, to meet them.
- Be enthusiastic about the group's goals and mission, about the individuals within the group, and about yourself.
- Allow people to make mistakes from which they can learn.
- Recogize and reward success or accomplishment, but don't be afraid to give negative feedback.
- Understand what people want for themselves and what they're willing to give in order to get what they want or need.
- Encourage cooperation within the group and reasonable competitiveness with other groups.
- Encourage productive disagreement while helping to resolve conflicts.

That's a lot of high-minded advice, isn't it? Sometimes, when you're dealing with people who seem not to care about anything, you think, "The heck with it. Fire 'em."

Well, that may be personally satisfying, but it's not the best management plan. The remaining chapters show you ways to get a handle on that advice not only by talking about motivation and motivating but also by modeling it.

Chapter 2

Jerry Barton: A Positive Role Model for Motivating Your Subordinates

Jerry Barton, a fictional person, is the model for how to handle employees who have the potential for doing more than they do or for producing higher-quality work but don't want to. Although cast as CPV Enterprises' new distribution center supervisor, he's a composite of many successful supervisors in many different fields. Jerry is a positive role model.

CPV (a medium-size mail order company) has hired Jerry to straighten up a mess left behind by a nonfunctioning, alcoholic supervisor. Jerry hasn't managed before this, but he has learned a lot about managing by working for a first-rate person. He has also just completed a two-year business program at the community college. This job will test the neat little theories he learned in Human Relations 101 and 102.

Among other nightmares left by his predecessor, he has inherited three employees who, as a result of no supervision, work totally without controls—when they work at all. He has permission to fire them, but the time and cost to replace these people makes that solution impractical: They know more about the inventory and the system (such as it is) than he could learn in several weeks on his own. No. His better judgment dictates that he try to straighten out the whole mess.

It's not that these people can't do their jobs. They just don't want to do them.

Take Janice. She started in the mail room six years ago, worked in receiving for three years, and here in the distribution center for two. But she won't lift a finger unless she's given explicit instructions. Withdrawn, sullen, and uncommunicative, Janice doesn't like managers very much.

Not that Jerry can blame her. The previous supervisor disliked working women, and he verbally abused her for anything she did—right or wrong. Why should she bother?

And Bud: A nicer, friendlier guy you'll never know—or want to. Bud chatters on nonstop about everything (whether or not he knows what he's talking about). All day he talks or sings or whistles or makes the funny noises he calls imitations. If you ask him to stop talking, he'll apologize profusely, shut up for five minutes, and then start over.

Difficult as those two employees are, neither presents the challenge Eddie does. Eddie labored a year in building maintenance before moving up to the center four years ago.

He's the "leader." Loud, boisterous, egocentric, he ran the center at its level of efficiency (such as *it* is) while Jones, his former boss, drank. Now, he resists direction and spends the day ordering Bud to do whatever work gets done while he sits at the shipping table, feet propped up, chair tilted backward precariously.

Jerry is supposed to turn this chaos into a productive environment, get these people to put in at least a day's work for a day's pay, and turn the distribution center into a profitable operation. To succeed, Jerry has to get the best he can from each person in his crew.

Now, while this particular story is fiction, all four people appear in abundance in the workplace. They're drawn from years of experience. As you read about them, see if anyone resembles someone you know.

You'll also be asked to do certain things: paper-and-pencil activities to help you rehearse ways of dealing with people whom you supervise. Application requires following the advice attributed to Confucius:

6

Tell me, and I forget.
Show me, and I remember.
Let me do, and I understand.

You'll learn by doing, not just by reading.

Jerry's Challenge

Jerry has met his employees once before, during the interview process. In the vending-machine room, over a Coke, they came across very differently from how they do as Jerry steps into his job. Everything Randy, his manager, has said about this motley crew appears to be true.

There's Eddie, sitting with his chair tilted back, feet up on a table, challenging Jerry to object. Bud's bustling about among the shelves singing some unintelligible song out of tune. Janice is sorting merchandise she has been removing from a large carton—one small piece at a time. The young supervisor can only wonder if he's really ready for this.

Well, it's a challenge, at any rate. Nothing else to do but to jump in:

Jerry: Mornin'. How's everyone?

        [*Eddie sits, Bud bustles and sings, and Janice silently sorts.*]

        Sorry I wasn't down here when you arrived this morning. Had to stop in Personnel. Fill out some forms and stuff.

        [*After ten or fifteen seconds of unresponsiveness, Jerry takes a different tack:*]

        Bud? Janice? Please stop what you're doing and join me and Eddie here at this table. I'd like to talk with you. Eddie. We need the table your feet are on.

        [*Eddie doesn't move.*]

        Take 'em down, please.

[*Eddie still doesn't move, so he adds an exclamation point.*]

Now!

[*The tone of voice gets a reaction. Eddie slowly removes his feet from the table and straightens up his chair and now slouches down in it, hands jammed into his pockets, jaw set.*]

Thank you.

Bud: [*Drawing up a chair*] How's the new boss?

Jerry: Fine. How are you?

Bud: As great as ever, especially now that someone's around here to control things again. Not having a real supervisor around was the pits. [*Those remarks are obviously aimed at Eddie.*]

Jerry: [*Aiming at the other man to see how he'll respond*] I understand Eddie had things running okay.

Eddie: You bet I did.

Bud: Well, maybe you can say Eddie held things together—in a way.

Jerry: Folks, I'm going to need your help. You know the stock, you know the inventory control system, you know the distribution procedures around here.

Eddie: I practically designed 'em myself.

Jerry: That's what you said the other day. I'll need you to review it all with me. Janice, I'll need your help, too. I saw you sorting some merchandise when I came in. I need to know what you do and how you do it. The same goes for you Bud. You seem to know where everything is, and—

Bud: That's for sure. The women's apparel starts right here and fills the first three aisles; men's apparel—

Eddie: [*Cutting in*] Not now, Jerko. I'll show 'im around later.

Jerry: Okay, fellas. Everyone will get a chance to show me what you do or have to show. We'll meet again to talk after I've caught up a bit, but, first, I'd like to say a few things.

I hear it was kinda rough on all of you. No details, but I understand Mr. Jones' personal problems affected everyone here. No standards, no goals, no controls—arbitrary, harsh. Things that make working conditions miserable.

Bud: [*Interrupting*] Jones drank too much. Booze for breakfast, lunch, supper, and coffee breaks. Came in stinko and yelled at everyone. Especially Jan. I almost decked him a couple of times.

Jerry: Thanks for the information, Bud. Let me reassure everyone, I drink only socially and usually only on the weekends. But all that's beside the point.

I want us to make this center profitable within the next six months. I know we can do it. It'll take some planning and some hard work. I won't know what it'll take till we go over the inventory reports and the distribution system and procedures.

Eddie: [*Sitting up straight in his chair*] Got you covered. I can handle the whole thing. Leave it up to me.

Jerry: I'll appreciate your help, Eddie. I'm looking forward to seeing what you've put in place here. I want us all to work out a complete plan together. I just want to say something that means a lot to me.

I expect a big effort from all of us, myself included. I have high standards, and I work hard to meet them. I expect everyone around me to do the same. I believe in myself and what I can do. I believe in you, also. I don't think anyone will let me down.

The last thing I want to say now is, I'm not the only one we'll let down by not doing our

9

jobs the best we can. It's all of us—you, me, Randy, the company.

It's like a football team. CPV's the team, and we're a specialty team—the kick return team. We either work together and score points, or we hurt ourselves and the team as a whole. If we score, we get the game ball.

I take the idea of teamwork seriously. I want you to take it that way, too. What do you say?

[*Looking at each other, everyone waits for someone else to speak.*]

Bud: [*True to fashion*] Sure, we'll give it a shot. You can count on us, can't he?

Eddie: [*Sitting up as tall as he can*] The company counts on me now, doesn't it? I won't let up just because they brought in someone else to run this outfit.

Jerry: [*Directing*] Janice? You haven't said anything at all.

[*The young woman blinks at her new supervisor, crosses her arms over her chest, and simply nods.*]

How do you feel about what I said?

Janice: Sounds okay.

Jerry: You in?

Janice: Yes.

Jerry: Thanks.

Chapter 3

How to Establish a Psychological Contract With the People You Supervise

In that little scene, Jerry does much more than give a pep talk. He establishes the norms that assert his authority. Quietly but firmly, he lets everyone know that he's in charge, that making the center profitable is his own wish. At the same time, he begins building the basis of a psychological contract: an unwritten agreement that spells out the supervisor's and the employee's mutual expectations, accountabilities, and consequences for success or failure.

In this step, Jerry follows the first bit of advice listed in Chapter 1. He has let everyone know he expects the best from all the people in the group, including himself.

Telling people that you expect the best from them means that you hold them accountable for meeting the high, but reasonable, standards on which you both agree. When you first hire someone, or each time you assign a new task to an employee, you both have to know what has to be done to reach the goals. They have to understand what you expect them to produce and in what manner. And you need to know what they expect you to do to make that work possible. Implied by those expectations are the results by which you both measure each other's effectiveness: your accountabilities.

Accountabilities

Accountabilities are the results you expect to get from the people whom you're trying to motivate: what has to

The Psychological Contract

- Mutual expectations
- Accountabilities
- Positive and negative consequences

---

be done, by whom, and what time (the deadlines). If they don't know what outcomes you're looking for, they certainly can't give them to you and you won't be able to recognize and reward success or accomplishment. As Jerry said to his group, "I want this center to become profitable within the next six months."

That's the group's objective. Jerry will also hold separate goal-setting meetings with each person as part of the firm's performance management/performance appraisal system.

Each person also has to know his or her individual responsibilities, even if, as in the case study, the group works together as a team. When other jobs depend on each person's completing his or her work, the accountabilities become especially important. Part of a person's motivation comes from knowing that he or she plays an important role in the organization, that other people count on him or her.

Jerry has made this point very clear:

Jerry: I believe in you. . . . I don't think anyone will let me down. . . . I'm not the only one we'll let down. . . . It's all of us—you, me, Randy, the company. It's like a football team. CPV's the team, and we're a specialty team—the kick return team. We either work together and score points, or we hurt ourselves and the team as a whole. If we score, we get the game ball.

After he made his speech, he tested the waters, checking to see if it reached anyone. They all agreed—or, at least, so they said.

Exploring Expectations

Soon Jerry will discuss with the group and each person in it their *mutual* expectations. He'll want to know from them what they expect of and from him as much as he'll want them to know what he expects.

Asking the right questions (open-ended ones, for the most part), he'll apply the old 20 percent rule: He'll talk only 20 percent of the time and allow the other people to talk the balance of it; he'll sit back and listen. That's the only way he'll find out what he wants to know. As long as he directs the discussion with appropriate questions and comments, Jerry will lead his employees to the conclusions, decisions, or plans that will most benefit the work group and the organization, as well as each individual.

The 20 percent rule accomplishes something else, too: When people do most of the talking, they feel involved, especially if they think you're really listening. They become much more enthusiastic about what they say than about what someone else tells them.

The rule also allows a person who knows what the job is and how to do it to take the lead. In later sections, Jerry will let Eddie clarify the details of his role and work out the details—but only after he reassures himself that his employee does in fact know how to control the inventory. Letting Eddie create his own job description will almost guarantee a commitment to living up to it.

The new manager will get his chance to talk, and when he does, he'll spell out his employees' tasks as he sees them. He'll work at spurring each person's desire to do his or her very best, and if he's successful, he'll reinforce that desire by pointing out the rewards a person will receive for a job well done.

People work for rewards. They don't have to be tangible, such as money. They can be intangible, as in the case of letting Eddie keep a leadership role in the group.

Jerry heard immediately that he would have to give Eddie a little responsibility or authority when the employee said, "Got you covered. . . . I can handle the whole thing. Leave it up to me." He heard it again later, when Eddie complained, "The company counts on me now, doesn't it? I won't let up just because they brought in someone else to run this outfit."

Making the Psychological Contract Work

Without four essential factors, Jerry and the others can't fulfill the psychological contract:

1. The people have to want to do their jobs and do them well.
2. They have to be capable of doing their jobs or learning how to do them.
3. They have to understand what they have to do and the standards by which their work will be judged.
4. There can be no obstacles or barriers to their performance.

In ordinary, everyday work environments, people come to work capable of doing the job and willing to do it well. Usually, the desire to do good work deteriorates and people become *de*motivated only if obstacles get in their way or if they don't understand what's expected of them or how their work will be evaluated.

Supervisors often create the most serious obstacles. Many make impossible demands while others make no demands at all. Many fail to provide the resources needed for doing the job (including their own availability). Some are not consistent in their expectations, changing them frequently. Many are too consistent in their expectations, inflexible and unable to cope with changing conditions in the work. Still others are not responsive to the employees' needs.

The employee's lack of skill or ability forms a barrier, while the organization erects barriers when it doesn't provide training, career opportunities, or appropriate rewards. All barriers demotivate employees. They give up trying, and many of them quit months before they leave the organization.

Additionally, not knowing the consequences for success or failure constitutes an important reason for people not giving their very best.

Consequences

When you hold someone accountable for something, you are responsible for explaining what happens if the job is or is not done successfully and who is affected and how. You must include the positive or negative consequences for the individual and also those for you, the group, and the organization—even, possibly, for the consumer of your goods or services—not just the team within the team, but rather the whole team and the people who depend on it count.

Your unit, just like Jerry's, is a specialty team that serves a function in the larger team—the organization. What each person does, be it for good or for ill, affects the whole team and its constituencies—employees, consumers, and the general public.

Jerry is trying to create a team environment by producing a psychological contract with the group as a whole before setting one up with each person in the group. (Separate discussions before he pulls the group together can generate more mistrust and apprehension than doing it the other way around.) He's telling everyone that he expects the same effort from each person, he's not making special deals with anyone.

He's letting the group know he has high standards that he expects everyone, including himself, to meet. He reassures them that he believes that they, as well as he, can rise to the challenges.

To get the most and the best from other people means that you must set high but reasonable standards, recognize your own accountabilities as well as the employee's, and let the employee either pay the price for messing up or be rewarded for succeeding.

Chapter 4

How to Use the Pygmalion Effect to Set High Standards

When you set high standards and let people know you believe in their ability to meet those standards, you become a Positive Pygmalion.

The Pygmalion Effect

Here's your chance to play Henry Higgins, of *My Fair Lady* (based on George Bernard Shaw's *Pygmalion*). Your employees can play the part of Eliza Doolittle, the cockney girl Higgins trains and passes off as a princess. The Pygmalion Effect is a term coming from the social psychologist's opinion that a manager is either a positive or negative change agent—a Pygmalion.

The name is drawn from the ancient Greek myth about the sculptor Pygmalion, who loved his statue and believed deeply in its beauty and goodness, wishing only that it could come to life. The goddess Athena, seeing how truly unselfish the artist's love was, fulfilled the wish.

It's not that easy for the modern manager. You have to work a little harder to exert sufficient influence and to encourage your employees to believe they can perform at peak levels. A Negative Pygmalion produces the exact opposite effect, and usually does it with little effort.

Positive Pygmalions begin by believing in themselves and in their ability to help and develop their employees. They communicate that self-confidence and their belief in the other people's capabilities. They then use those beliefs as self-fulfilling prophecies. They work to make those beliefs come true.

When the Pygmalion does what's necessary to help ensure success, the other people make a real effort to live up to his faith in them. In the final analysis, the Pygmalion rewards the people by believing in them and by helping them "make it." By succeeding, they reward their mentor.

Jerry has begun the process by sharing with them his faith in the group. He intends to carry that forward to each individual as time goes along.

Setting High but Reasonable Standards

You can't get the best out of people if you don't expect the best from them. Although expecting it won't automatically produce it, not expecting it usually produces a negative outcome.

Also, you can't expect the best from people if you don't tell them that you expect it. Accountabilities and high standards constitute the heart of the Positive Pygmalion's psychological contract.

In the process of spelling out the accountabilities, you also work with the employees to establish mutually acceptable standards of performance.

You use this opportunity to motivate people by involving them, by letting them tell you what they think they can do. In many management studies, employees complain that their supervisors don't expect enough from them. These studies show that the employees tend to expect more of and set higher standards for themselves than their supervisors do.

Often, when supervisors collaborate on setting goals and standards, they have to help their employees look at them more realistically than some do. Still, you don't want to pull anyone too far back from his or her own goals. People are more likely to commit themselves to decisions they make than to decisions you make for them. Since veteran employees usually know what to do and how to do it, and they usually take pride in their work, letting them set their own standards is particularly motivating.

The most effective way of getting the best from people is to let them reach for increasingly higher standards, to stretch themselves to accomplish more or do better in their jobs—to compete with themselves against a standard instead of measuring themselves against what other people do. To get the results you want, emphasize flexible, objective, and realistic performance standards, individual behaviors in relation to standards, and the benefits to the individual for achieving them. Flexibility and realism come with setting performance ranges rather than making a one-shot demand, all or nothing.

The sidebar on this page illustrates a performance range in which new employees or trainees are expected to perform at a minimum or basic level and in which, after a period of time, employees are expected to exceed that minimum. The step after minimum requirements is called reasonable expectations—what a well-trained, experienced employee is expected to produce in a given period of time without undue fatigue.

Standards measure the quantity and quality of work produced over time. By studying past history in the job, current conditions, and the employees' skill levels, you can decide what is a high but reasonable expectation for any well-trained, experienced employee. Anyone who exceeds 100 percent of that standard becomes your "superstar," and that's the level you encourage people to reach.

In the beginning, you can expect a new employee or a trainee to perform at a level below minimum expec-

- -

Performance Range

Over 100%	Exceeds reasonable expectations
85%–100%	Meets reasonable expectations
70%–84%	Meets minimum requirements of the job
Under 70%	Performs below minimum requirements

- -

tations in both quantity and quality of work (less than 70 percent of the standards). With orientation or training, he or she will first work very deliberately to improve the *quality* of work before producing the quantity of work expected of trained employees. It takes time, and you need patience. You also have to decide on how much time it should take for an employee to begin producing an acceptable quantity of work. Decide, too, at what point in time less than 70 percent of standard becomes unacceptable. At that time, you may have to ask the employee to accept a transfer (if one is possible) or leave the organization. You can't expect the best from everyone if you allow one person to perform consistently at less than the minimum standard.

The time to ask for the best from people is when you're negotiating and clarifying roles, something you should do fairly regularly.

Negotiating and Clarifying Roles

Negotiating and clarifying roles with people motivates them; it shows you're interested in what they do. Your effort lets them know that you believe that what they do is important enough for you to take the time to discuss their work with them. It also indicates that you recognize that work conditions change, that jobs change with them, and that the standards change as well.

By discussing your role as well as the employees', you share responsibility for seeing to it that they succeed. They, in turn, feel a need to exceed expectations or to accept additional work when necessary.

You perform your role by giving direction to the employees as you monitor their work. You don't lay out all the details, do their work for them, or solve their problems. Instead, by encouraging people to solve their own problems, you allow them to take responsibility for their own performance. You allow them the independence, autonomy, and self-esteem they need for giving their very best.

At the same time, monitoring their work allows you

to prevent problems from becoming crises. You can act proactively (as opposed to reactively) to any deviation from goals and standards you spot. That's built into your accountabilities as a supervisor.

Your goal is to help people take responsibility for what they do and for what they get in return for what they do.

It's been a while since you last saw what was going on at CPV Enterprises' distribution center. Let Jerry illustrate how to be a Positive Pygmalion.

Chapter 5

Jerry as a Positive Pygmalion

Jerry has been on the job a few days now, reviewing inventory reports, stock manuals, management control reports, and financial data. He's had Bud take him on a tour (much to Eddie's disgust), and watched the three people in action (or inaction, as was often the case). It's time for him to begin negotiating and clarifying roles, starting with Eddie—the leader.

In this segment of dialogue, the young manager uses encouragement to win Eddie's support. He encourages and allows the employee to express all his feelings. He doesn't use compliments or flattery to win him over. Instead, he used openness and friendliness.

Jerry also involves Eddie, draws him out. If you have the time to count words, see how many more of Eddie's you read than Jerry's.

Jerry Wins Over Eddie

Jerry: I appreciate your coming in to talk with me, Eddie. I think it's time we got to know each other better.

Eddie: Guess so. Seems like you spend most of your time in here or out on the floor with Bud.

Jerry: You think I'm spending more time with Bud than with you.

Eddie: Yeah.

Jerry: And you don't like that.

Eddie: [*Flushing a little*] Well, when you put it that way, it sounds kinda childish, doesn't it?

Jerry: Does it?

Eddie: It does to me. I guess I'm a little jealous, but I suppose you need to find out where everything is, and since Bud's put it all there, he's the logical one to talk to.

Jerry: [*Leaning forward on his desk, wishing he had a larger office with more than one side chair—He doesn't even have room to move his chair out from behind the desk, which he feels sets up a barrier.*] I'm glad you see it that way. Now that I know what we have and where it all is, I'd like to find out how we keep track of it. You tell me you're my man.

Eddie: Yeah, I am. I built the system from scratch. We had nothing, and Jones didn't care any more. He did, once, when the company was very small. When we opened new territories, they brought me in here. That's when Jones began drinking during the day. He couldn't keep up with it, and he knew I could take away his job some day. [*Eddie stops, realizing what he has just said.*] Well, he's gone, but I didn't take his job away from him.

Jerry: You wanted it, didn't you?

Eddie: Sure. Wouldn't you? [*Laughing*] I guess you do.

Jerry: I do, and I appreciate that you do, too. [*He can genuinely empathize.*] If I were you, I'd probably not like me right now.

Eddie: It's not that I don't like you. It's just that I think I can do it. I don't understand why they didn't give me a chance. They said it's because I don't know anything about computers. What's that supposed to mean?

Jerry: [*Surprised by the question—Doesn't Eddie know?*] We plan to automate the system.

Eddie: How?

Jerry: Put inventory control into a computer, tie distribution and shipping in with sales, billing, and accounting.

Eddie: I could learn it.

Jerry: You're angry about being passed over.

Eddie: You bet I am. I could've learned the system! [*Fighting back his disappointment and giving up some of his anger*] I'm not mad at you. I suppose I'm angry at myself for not going to school like you did. You know the system, and that gives you a leg up on me.

Jerry: I suppose so.

Eddie: With your training, you can help design the new system. I can't do what you can.

Jerry: Yes, but I need your help to do it.

Eddie: [*Now surprised*] Me? What for?

Jerry: You know the manual system. We have to translate it for the computer.

Eddie: I don't get it. What can I do?

Jerry: I don't know. You tell me.

Eddie: What's this? A game?

Jerry: No. I'm serious. I need your help. You want to help, and neither of us is sure what you can do, but you know what you know. That may be the best place to start.

Eddie: Well, yeah. I guess—I suppose I'd better teach you what I did here.

Jerry: I need to know that.

Eddie: I put together the inventory control system and the shipping procedures. Set up the connection between us and billing. Well, not all by myself. Marva, in accounting, helped me with the billing. And, I guess Bud helped me with the inventory. And Jan's been a good soldier. Man, she's had it bad here. I don't know why she stuck it out. You talk with her yet?

Jerry: Not much. I will, soon. But for now, let's talk about inventory control. Seems to me you put together a pegboard system.

Eddie: Yeah. That's right. I read about it in a magazine that Jones had here. A two-part article. It said that a pegboard system helps you track. . . .

What Did Jerry Do?

Take a piece of paper and list the ways Jerry encouraged Eddie to talk. You should find as many as nine different things Jerry did or said.

When you're finished, turn to the list of the encouragers Jerry used shown in Exhibit 1. Then continue your reading.

Jerry Wins Over Jan

Jerry has no problem getting Bud's support, and you'll see how later he gets Bud to stop distracting everyone else.

No, these two present only minor problems. Jerry's most serious problem is winning over Jan. He sees and feels her hostility and wariness. Let's see how he handles the situation:

Exhibit 1. Jerry's encouragers for Eddie.

1. He expressed appreciation.
2. He expressed a desire to know the other person.
3. He let Eddie talk about his feelings regarding the time he spent with Bud without judging those feelings.
4. He leaned forward on his desk to be as close to Eddie as space allowed.
5. He acknowledged Eddie's role in designing the manual system and satisfied Eddie's need to be recognized.
6. He let Eddie talk about his feelings about not getting the job, and empathized with him.
7. He gave Eddie honest answers.
8. He invited Eddie to help design the new system.
9. He listened, giving undivided attention, at all times.

Jan:	[*Tapping on the doorframe*] You want to see me?
Jerry:	[*Looking up from the ledger in which he is writing*] Give me a second to finish or I'll lose my place. Then I can put away the books. Okay?
Jan:	[*Sitting down, crossing her arms*] Sure.

[*Jerry enters a column of numbers, closes the ledger, and puts it and some papers into a desk drawer.*]

Jerry:	Thanks for coming in to talk.
Jan:	What about?
Jerry:	To get to know each other better, find out what you've been doing, what you'd like to do. Things like that.
Jan:	Okay. Talk.
Jerry:	Hear it's been pretty rough around here. What happened? [*Jan clearly doesn't want to answer.*] Guess that was too direct. Let's start with whatever you'd like to talk about.
Jan:	Why?
Jerry:	I'm serious about wanting to know you better.
Jan:	What for?
Jerry:	So we can work together more effectively.
Jan:	I don't understand what you want from me. I'll do my work. Just tell me what to do.
Jerry:	You seem pretty angry with me.
Jan:	[*Pausing. Then, more subdued*] Can I go back to work now?
Jerry:	Sure. I think I understand how you feel. See you later!

Jan exits the office, leaving Jerry disturbed by his clumsiness and puzzled about what to do next. For the next few days, he does what Jan has asked of him: he tells her what to do and thanks her for doing it, giving her no special attention or praise for doing what she is supposed to do anyway. He doesn't try to avoid her, but he doesn't invade her privacy, either.

In a few days, Jerry notices some change. Jan's tone of voice has softened, she doesn't glare at him as much and doesn't sit with her arms crossed. Little victories mean a lot.

Nearly a month later, Jan knocks on the doorframe again.

Jan: Busy? Can I come in?

Jerry: Please. These reports are pretty dull, anyway.

Jan: [*Sitting down, and without ceremony*] No, you don't understand.

Jerry: I'm sorry, but what don't I understand?

Jan: You said that day you think you understand. No, you don't.

Jerry: I see. Want to tell me about it?

Jan: Not really, but I guess I oughta show you that much courtesy. What do you want to know?

Jerry: [*Leaning on his desk*] Jan, I don't want to know anything you don't want to tell me. I want us to work together well. I heard you had it rough, and I want to reassure you that whatever happened won't happen again.

Jan: I believe you. I'm sorry I've been mean to you, not giving you a chance. Jones gave me a bad time, and I'd rather forget about it.

Jerry: That's fine with me.

Jan: He treated me like a backward child and chewed me out for everything, even for things that happened when I wasn't there. Why should I trust you?

Jerry: Good point.

[*They sit in silence for a few moments.*]

Jan: Well, I'm beginning to trust you—a little. I still need to wait and see. Now, what do you want from me? I mean it this time.

Jerry: First, I want to apologize to you, too. I was too direct. I said so then because I realized it immediately. I'm sorry for that.

Jan: Oh, that's okay. I realize you meant no harm. I shouldn't have been so up tight about it.

Jerry: Jan, all I need from you is good, honest work. I've learned a little about what you do, but it's only the things I've told you to do, the mini-

	mum requirements of the job. I think you've more to offer, and I'd like to see it. Since I've a ways to go to earn your trust, I won't push you for anything, but I want you to know what I think. How do you feel about that?
Jan:	About what?
Jerry:	That you've more to offer than the bare minimum.
Jan:	Well, sure. You don't expect me to argue with that, do you?
Jerry:	I hope not.
Jan:	C'mon. Let's stop jockeying around. I think I'm ready to listen to you.
Jerry:	Well, I'm ready to listen to you, too.

What Did Jerry Do?

Review the dialogue with Jan, the way you did the one with Eddie, to see the ten ways Jerry won Jan's support. When you're finished, check your answers against Exhibit 2. Then, continue reading.

Jerry gave direction to his employees, he didn't order them to do anything or lay out all the details of their jobs or of their relationship to him. He encouraged them to solve their own problems and allowed them to take responsibility for their own performance, at all times reaffirming their needs for independence, autonomy, and self-esteem—needs everyone has to meet.

Chapter 6

And Now for a Little Theory: The Importance of Recognizing Needs

No one does anything without a reason, and when people come to your organization, they come motivated—pleased that they got the job, eager to do well, and ready to work. Getting the job has satisfied whatever needs they had for applying in the first place: money, opportunity, challenge, or the social climate. Whatever the reason, they're glad to be there.

At the same time, the whole person comes to work, bringing along personal as well as work-related needs and interests. When people feel that someone else or the organization rides over their needs or frustrates their interests, motivation on the job becomes a problem. Eddie's resentment over not getting promoted and Jan's anger over Jones' mistreatment both illustrate the point.

People are goal-directed. They need to realize a benefit or payoff to feel good about what they do. Although few people carefully think out their motives or reasons, and often don't understand them even when they know they're there, a motive or reason hides behind whatever they do.

People don't always know what's pushing or pulling them until they act on their motives. They feel a discomfort, a lack of something, a need they have to meet—and they work hard to reduce the discomfort or to fill the need. *That's what motivation's all about.*

Some motives, such as Bud's need to be everyone's friend, have the force of drivers. They are compulsions

Exhibit 2. Jerry's encouragers for Jan.

1. He expressed appreciation.
2. He admitted his mistake when he was too direct.
3. He nonjudgmentally allowed her to express her feelings.
4. He respected her privacy when she refused to discuss her past situation.
5. He reassured her through actions rather than through words that he would not abuse her.
6. He let her come to him.
7. He accepted her apology and apologized also.
8. He expressed his confidence in her abilities.
9. He was honest with her.
10. He listened, giving undivided attention, at all times.

for acting that, left unsatisfied, make a person very uncomfortable. Abraham Maslow, developer of the best-known motivation theory, describes a hierarchy of five such basic drives: physiological, safety, social, ego, and self-fulfillment needs.

According to Maslow, people first take care of basic survival needs, such as food and shelter. After meeting those physical needs, they strive to satisfy safety or security needs: protection from harm. Once those needs are met, they seek out the company of others: giving and getting love and affection, sympathy, and caring.

Beyond those needs, people satisfy drives related to self-esteem or ego needs: taking on challenges, seeking recognition and attention from others, attempting to lead. Finally, when all those needs are met, they can look into themselves for achievement, for self-satisfaction, for understanding and knowledge—personal growth for its own sake. That, at least, is how Maslow views things.

Since the 1960's, a number of people have modified the theory. Henry A. Murray, for example, drops Maslow's concern for physiological drives and expands the list of needs to thirteen, as shown in the sidebar. He deemphasizes physiological drives, partly because he sees needs as essentially *learned* behaviors stimulated by cues from the outside rather than from inside a person.

Murray's view differs from Maslow's in several ways. Although most of his categories track with Maslow's definitions of the five basic needs, the new definitions are more specific and focus more on extremes of behavior. For example, Murray treats autonomy as a demand for complete freedom and separateness, whereas Maslow refers to it as a need for independence of thought and action. To these drivers, he adds the need for power, which Maslow omitted. Maslow says that each lower level of need must be satisfied in order to satisfy the higher levels, but Murray thinks you can satisfy different needs at the same time, either to the same degree of satisfaction or to lesser or greater degrees. Finally, Murray says a person's personality consists of these diverse, often conflicting, needs.

I agree with Murray that you can probably break needs up into more than five categories, but disagree with the theory that all needs come from acquired behavior. I also agree with Murray that you can satisfy

- -

Murray's Categories of Needs

Self-Fulfillment Needs
Achievement, endurance, understanding

Social Needs
Affiliation, giving or getting sympathy, love, affection

Ego Needs
Exhibitionism, aggressiveness, impulsiveness, independence, autonomy

Safety Needs
Avoidance of harm, a need for order

Power Needs
Control

- -

more than one need at a time, regardless of where in the hierarchy they fall. And I break with both Murray and Maslow on the issue of personal power.

Instead of calling personal power an ego need (Maslow) or a separate and distinct need (Murray), I think that "personal power" refers to:

> The competence of adults to meet their own needs, whatever the need may be—e.g., security, achievement, and social belonging. . . .

People feel their need for personal power is fulfilled only when they believe they have satisfied some need through their own efforts or talents: "I Did It My Way." The popular song title sums it all up very well. When you believe that someone or something denies you power over your life, you feel debased and demeaned, robbed of your dignity. That's a point the Eddie and Jan cases describe.

On the other hand, the case of former supervisor Jones illustrates how a person can carry the exercise of personal power to extremes, especially in the service of ego needs. He tried to satisfy his ego needs at the expense of or to the detriment of other people. He exercised his personal power to bully Jan. When line employees throw their weight around, conflict usually breaks out. When managers do it, demotivation destroys the unit's effectiveness.

You can't really know what payoffs drive another person. At best, you can observe his or her behavior, make an educated guess, and check it out. You could give recognition for work well done to someone like Eddie, who seems driven by ego needs. Or you could protect the safety needs of a person like Jan, who runs for cover no matter how well he or she performs. And so forth.

Reinforcing Motivation With Incentives

You saw in Chapters 3 and 4 (the psychological contract and the Pygmalion Effect) that a person begins a job with the desire to do it. Yet, desire in itself doesn't guarantee that someone will do his or her very best. That desire has to be reinforced.

The ideas of the psychological contract and the Pygmalion Effect fit together with another theory of motivation, this one developed by L. L. Cummings and D. P. Schwab: *expectancy* theory. In simplest terms, the theory says that the more people value the payoff they expect for their efforts, the more likely they are to do their best. Of course, successful performance still depends on a person's having the ability to do the job and seeing his or her role clearly.

All these theories refer to rewards or reinforcement—need satisfiers and incentives. Without them motivation dies. In your workplace, you control rewards, especially the intangible ones such as recognition. According to Frederick Herzberg, those rewards take two forms: hygiene factors (maintenance) and motivation factors.

Hygiene factors consist of the quality of working conditions, effective supervision, equitable company policies, and fair administration. The absence of these rewards *dis*satisfy employees; their absence *de*motivates. Their presence keeps employees feeling good about the organization and the work group, but they don't really do much to motivate. After all, they're simply the payoffs—need satisfiers—employees *expect* to find in return for their work.

Herzberg then said that genuine motivation arises from advancement, responsibility, challenging work, recognition, and achievement. These essentially intangible rewards provide incentives that produce job satisfaction. They reinforce the employees' motivation, primarily in terms of self-esteem and a sense of personal power. In this respect, Herzberg agrees with those who champion the reinforcement theory of motivation.

E. E. Adams, for example, claims that you can modify someone's behavior by using rewards for doing the work well or for behaving in accordance with company goals, standards, and norms. Rewards that satisfy real needs provide reinforcement through frequent positive feedback.

Herzberg's Satisfiers and Motivators

> *Hygiene Factors*
> Working Conditions
> Supervision
> Interpersonal relations
> Salary
> Equitable company policies
> Fair administration
>
> *Motivators*
> Advancement
> Responsibility
> Challenging work
> Recognition
> Achievement

For example, if you're delegating a job and want that person to do his or her very best, you're pretty likely to get it if you set goals and standards and divide the job you delegate into smaller objectives. By rewarding the person at each step, you're rewarding him or her for many successful achievements rather than for just one. Little successes then breed big successes.

At the same time, you have to fit the rewards to the person. The right reward for the wrong person could produce negative effects instead of positive reinforcement. Jerry reinforces his group members' feelings about themselves and about what they want out of their work, moving them from downright hostility toward cooperation. He motivates them.

As with most useful psychological concepts, each theory—Maslow's and Murray's needs theory, Cummings' and Schwab's expectancy theory, Herzberg's reward theory, and Adams' reinforcement theory—has something to offer. Yet any one theory, taken by itself, won't help you all that much when you try to get the best from other people. Motivation may or may not come from within, but the rewards—the incentives—

most frequently come from outside. That's why you want to combine the motivation theories with ideas about rewards and other forms of reinforcement.

The needs theories call attention to contents: *what* specific needs you have. The expectancy theory calls attention to process: *how* a person is motivated. The reward and reinforcement theories call attention to what *incentives* may work and how they can be used. They all have more practical application when used together than when used separately.

The integration of theories results in three things:

1. A way of talking about the needs people usually try to meet
2. An understanding of how people usually try to meet their needs
3. An ability to identify the payoffs people seek from you or the organization for their efforts

Take a look at just a few of the ways you can pull these ideas together and make decisions about how to encourage people and help keep them motivated.

Herzberg's list of dissatisfiers and satisfiers fits with the drives described by Maslow and Murray. Working conditions and salary correlate with physiological needs and safety. Company policy and supervision relate to safety needs as well. Interpersonal relations relate to social needs. All the satisfiers correlate with ego needs, and achievement correlates with self-fulfillment.

Likewise, both the needs and the rewards correlated fit with typical worker expectations. Employees expect working conditions to be safe, clean, and accommodating. They expect salary, supervision, and company policies and administration to be fair and in accordance with the agreements set up when they hired on. The psychological contract generates expectations with regard to advancement, responsibility, the challenge of the work, recognition, and the opportunity for achievement. By integrating the diverse viewpoints, you can evaluate how well you or the organization are living up to the contract.

Each time you or the organization meets one of

those expectations, the reward reinforces the person's desire to repeat the successful performance that netted him or her the expected and valued result. Failure to meet the expectations results in demotivation and the loss of productivity, if not the loss of the producer. What reinforcers are you or the organization providing?

When you pull together all these theories, you have a thoroughgoing guide for finding ways to stimulate your people to do their very best. It boils down to recognizing that everyone looks to their work for payoffs that meet their needs. They expect the organization and you to fulfill the contract formed when they agreed to come to work and you agreed to hire them.

Answering the question of what drives you can help you understand what drives your employees to work. They probably want to meet needs very similar to yours. People really aren't that much different from each other. Rather, everyone exhibits relatively predictable patterns of behavior that reflect basic human needs they hope to meet either through tangible or intangible payoffs. They most frequently seek or respond to those rewards with the greatest payoff.

Can you apply these integrated content and process theories of motivation to yourself? What rewards satisfy the needs that drive you to work? What payoffs do you want from your work? Before moving on, look at the payoffs listed in Exhibit 3 and try to answer those questions for yourself.

Exhibit 3. Payoffs that people often seek from their work.

The list below consists of 17 possible reasons that people have for working. Each word or phrase can be used to answer the question, "What do I want to get out of the effort I'm putting into my work?"

1. *Knowledge:* To pursue and learn about new things and ideas; to search for truth, or information; to be known by others as an intelligent person and feel intelligent.

2. *Power:* To lead and direct others; to influence or control others, i.e., to get them to do what I want them to do.
3. *Independence:* To achieve my own goals in the manner best suited to me; to have freedom to come and go as I wish; to be myself at all times; to control my own actions.
4. *Accomplishment:* To achieve my personal objectives with a sense that I've done something as well as, if not better than, someone else; to experience self-satisfaction when I rise to a challenge, accomplish a task or a job, or solve a problem.
5. *Recognition:* To receive attention, notice, approval, or respect from others because of something I've done; to generate a feeling in others for who I am and what I achieve.
6. *Friendship:* To have many friends; to work with others and enjoy their camaraderie; to join groups for companionship; to look forward to and enjoy social relations.
7. *Responsibility:* To be held accountable to others or to organizations to which I belong for a job or task; to possess something and care for it.
8. *Creativity:* To have the ability, desire, and freedom to develop new ideas, solutions to problems, improvements in products or procedures, or designs of things or plans; to be mentally challenged; to be first to innovate or create.
9. *Security:* To possess the basic wherewithal for living; to feel safe; to have self-confidence; to have job security and continuity of income.
10. *Dedication:* To be loyal to the company or my supervisor, my family, social and political groups, and others; to give devotion, commitment, or friendship to others.
11. *Justice and parity:* To receive rewards and recognition for my contributions and achievements in proportion to my effort and comparable with those received by other people.

(continued)

Exhibit 3. (*continued*)

12. *Growth:* To advance, to expand my life through my job and through the improvement of my status at work or in the community; to increase my work- and nonwork-related knowledge or skills; to find fulfillment in the groups in which I work or live; to mature personally and professionally.
13. *Self-esteem:* To be someone of value in my own and other people's eyes; to be accepted as a person instead of a nonentity or a means to an end; to feel useful and wanted by other people; to be a leader; to be appreciated by others.
14. *Challenge:* To feel good about what I do, its degree of difficulty, and the complexity or demands on my creativity; to have opportunities to apply my knowledge and skills effectively and easily.
15. *Helpfulness:* To provide assistance, support, empathy, or protection to others; to be open, responsive, and generous.
16. *Money:* To have sufficient income or other assets to use as I wish; to be materially comfortable or well off.
17. *Good times/pleasure:* To have fun; to enjoy myself; to do the things I like to do instead of only the things I have to do.

You may want to pick up another book in this series, *How To Manage Stress.* It has a self-evaluation tool in the back that could help you look at your most important motivators. For the time being, check out the list on these few pages. It consists of seventeen of the most common payoffs people seek from their work. How many of them would meet your needs? How many would meet the needs of your subordinates?

Chapter 7

Using Autonomy and Rewards to Spur Success

By allowing people to exercise their autonomy, they *earn* the rewards they get. They also deserve *not* getting rewards when they don't perform up to standards. You make their rewards available, but they're in control of whether they get them, not you. So, how can you encourage autonomy and at the same time be responsible for making rewards available?

Autonomy

Maslow, Murray, and Herzberg all agree that allowing employees autonomy and personal power helps create a productive environment.

Some managers supervise employees too closely, believing that since they're the managers, they have to guide the people in each phase of the work. But when managers spoonfeed employees, they deny themselves two important resources: (1) creative employees and (2) their own time. They wind up solving the employees' problems and doing their work for them. What a waste.

From the employees' standpoint, it's also a waste. People want to meet their ego or self-fulfillment needs by owning the autonomy to choose whether or not to meet their standards. Instead of feeling grateful to their managers for helping, adults who feel spoonfed become resentful and rebellious. At best, they turn off and become increasingly demotivated. The turnover eats a manager's time and budget as no other problem can.

Another group—perfectionist managers—damage autonomy by making standards that are too high and demanding nothing less than 100 percent. They demotivate their employees, first by setting unachievable, unrealistic goals; next by intolerance, allowing for no mistakes from which people might learn and grow; and finally, by inflexibility, often requiring that the work be done only as they say it should. An unproductive sea of tension and stress swallows up each individual in the group.

Watch how Jerry encourages autonomy by giving Bud a chance to change his distracting and annoying behavior without telling him exactly what to do or making outrageous demands. By getting Bud's viewpoint before he expresses his own, resolving a disagreement, and assuming appropriate responsibilities for helping, he leads Bud into devising a plan for change.

Bud appears at the office door.

Jerry: C'mon in. I appreciate your taking a few minutes to talk with me.

Bud: Hey. No problem. Whatever the boss wants, the boss gets.

Jerry: How've you been?

Bud: Never better. Thanks to you. You sure have things running like they've never been before. Gotta give you a lotta credit.

Jerry: I appreciate that, Bud, but you know I couldn't have gotten this much done without you three. At the same time, we have a long way to go. Work out a few small problems, as well.

Bud: [*His smile freezing*] I suppose that's why you wanted to see me.

Jerry: [*Reassuring*] Not a major problem, but one that we should work on together. Several times, I've asked you to keep your mind on your work and to lower the noise level. A few times lately, I've heard you and Eddie arguing—

Bud: [*Interrupting*] He's just bossing me around again.

38

Jerry: What's happening?

Bud: He's always on me about something. He yells at me about wasting time, making unnecessary noise, too much chatter—like he's my boss.

Jerry: You don't think he should talk to you about those things.

Bud: Well, no. You're my boss, not him.

Jerry: Why do you think he's complaining?

Bud: Just bossing me around, like he's always done.

Jerry: You don't think you waste time, make unnecessary noise, or chatter too much.

Bud: Well, maybe I do—sometimes. Like you said, you've talked to me about it a couple of times. I've cut it way back, haven't I?

Jerry: I'm really interested in what *you* think, Bud. Do *you* think you've cut it "way back"?

Bud: Yeah. Don't you think so?

Jerry: If you're ready to listen to my opinion, I'll answer your question. What do you say?

Bud: Sure, I'm ready. I asked for it.

Jerry: I think you've cut back, but I don't think you've cut "*way* back," and though I don't think Eddie should "boss you" around, I think he has the right to talk to you about it if it annoys him. How do you feel about what I said?

Bud: [*Angry*] I thought I cut way back.

Jerry: Just this morning, I asked you twice to concentrate on work and wait till lunch to talk about the game last night. [*Continuing without any anger in his voice*] Yesterday, late in the day, I heard Eddie tell you that he was trying to learn how to use the PC. Your imitations distracted him. Does that seem like cutting "*way* back"?

Bud: I'm sorry, Jerry. I'll cut it out altogether. I really will.

Jerry: I know you'll try, and I'm glad to hear it. Let's see how we can change this situation permanently. What do you think we can do?

Bud: I don't know.

Jerry: Well, let's talk it over. Why do you interrupt people and sing or do your imitations so much?

Bud: I enjoy it, I guess. [*Hesitating*] They get me attention is probably more like it.

Jerry: The attention you're getting isn't the most favorable.

Bud: I guess that's a darn good reason for cutting it out.

Jerry: Could be. If you do cut it out, you'll have a much better relationship with all of us. If you don't cut it out, we may have to talk about a transfer.

Bud: That's kinda stiff. [*Taking a deep breath*] I suppose it's worse than I thought, but I like the job, and I think we're shaping up. I'd rather work on the problem than a transfer.

Jerry: Now, I can help you by asking Eddie to stop shouting at you and by keeping my eye on how you're doing, but you've got to do it yourself. You need a plan for change. Okay?

Bud: Sure.

Jerry: If you think you'd like more attention—more positive attention—what do you think you can do?

What Did Jerry Do?

Bud will give Jerry some good ideas, but it's not necessary to go into them in detail. What Jerry did is more important.

Review the dialogue with Bud, the way you did those with Eddie and Jan, to see the fourteen ways Jerry encouraged Bud to give more attention to solving the problem. When you're finished, check your answers against ours in Exhibit 4. Then, continue reading.

As you saw, until now, Jerry allowed Bud the chance to change on his own. He gave him the opportunity to make mistakes and learn from them, as well. Since the problem persisted, he had to take corrective action by encouraging Bud to see reality from other people's perspectives and to work on solving the problem.

Exhibit 4. Jerry's encouragers with Bud.

1. He expressed appreciation.
2. He gave credit for good work.
3. He gave Bud chances to change behavior before taking firm action.
4. He nonjudgmentally detailed the problem.
5. He let Bud know that he had confidence in him to do good work and to solve this problem.
6. He took responsibility for *helping* to solve the problem.
7. He was honest with Bud.
8. He disputed Bud's perception of the situation without judging him.
9. He reassured Bud that he would help.
10. He gave immediate, specific, and accurate feedback.
11. He mentioned both positive and negative consequences.
12. He let Bud choose whether or not to do something about the situation.
13. He let Bud design the plan.
14. He listened, giving undivided attention, at all times.

Once again, Jerry gave direction to another person, instead of ordering him to do something or laying out all the details of a plan. He encouraged Bud to solve his own problem and allowed him to take responsibility for his own performance, at all times reaffirming Bud's independence, autonomy, and self-esteem.

If you allow people autonomy and personal power and they reach their goals, they earn the rewards they expect. If they fail, they don't get those rewards. They're accountable. It's up to them.

Rewarding for Success

Allowing people to exercise their autonomy and holding them accountable for their actions also define your role more clearly. Decisions to reward and what to provide as reinforcements flow from the psychological contract and follow on the heels of objective and clear-cut data, such as production reports. Personal relationships or other subjective factors won't cut it, and if everyone knows you won't reward them on that basis, they won't demand it of you.

Rewards for good performance are among the positive consequences that you spell out through the psychological contract. Many managers make these terms of the contract very explicit because they don't control delivery of some rewards people want. It's not always easy to match rewards to needs.

Yet to work effectively, the promised rewards have to match the needs of the individual. The individual has to see the value of those rewards to him- or herself, not just how the organization benefits by what he or she does. Rewards become positive reinforcers when they meet specific needs of the individual.

Even though supervisors don't always control rewards—especially tangible rewards such as money—they must supply incentives to get the best from people. That is when supervisors become cheerleaders.

As Herzberg said, the absence of effective technical and personal supervision is a dissatisfier. Feedback from you, both positive and negative, plays an important role—probably the most essential feature of the reinforcement process. Positive feedback supports the effort that goes into doing the job and doing it well. Negative feedback leads to corrective action, preventing the person from going too far astray.

Letting the person know how he or she is doing gives the person the feeling that you take seriously what he or she does. You're paying attention to both the person and the work. All this enhances the person's self-esteem and feelings of importance. But praise alone is not the only necessary reinforcer. The organization has to make tangible rewards available as well.

Sometimes, the people Maslow called self-actualizers take all the reinforcement they need from the performance records they keep on their own work and progress. These records give self-validating feedback about their work and about how well they're doing. It's an "attaboy" or "attagirl" that the employee can *see*.

On the other hand, most people need reinforcement from outside themselves—recognition or some other positive reinforcement—when performance matches or exceeds expectations. They need support and encouragement when it doesn't.

Although praise is most often the most practical positive reinforcer, you can't always count on it to work with everyone, and praise for doing a job far beneath the person's capabilities is faint indeed. Additional money is important. People look to their work to earn their income, and they expect it in return for doing their jobs; also, they expect to receive more income when they do well at their work and exceed expectations. But using money to motivate means more to the managers than it usually does to their employees.

Motivation induced by money dies shortly after the people receive the raise. The additional income loses its effect within a matter of days, sometimes within hours, unless you use genuine drivers to motivate people.

Payoffs that meet the individual's own needs or goals are genuine drivers. To be appropriate, as opposed to being a form of manipulation or insincere bribes, the promised rewards must satisfy at least five criteria.

1. Rewards should be given only for successfully completing a task that meets real needs of the organization, of the manager, and of the individual.
2. Promised rewards must match the needs of the individual.
3. Rewards must be deliverable.
4. Rewards have to be accessible and immediate, not vague promises.
5. Rewards should fit with the previous experience people have had with the organization.

Encouragers acknowledge work that meets minimum standards (ho-hum work rates a ho-hum re-

Examples of Rewards Tailored to Specific Needs

- *Challenging work:* As a result of feelings of self-esteem, a sense of pride, and a need to stretch mentally, many people want to do more than what they perceive as mundane or dull or menial tasks. More interesting work (not just more of the same) rewards them.
- *Social recognition:* For some people, praise is not enough. They feel rewarded when recognized by the group or at least when recognized in front of it. (At the same time, other people feel uneasy with this.)
- *Opportunities for leadership:* Most nonmanagers have few chances to take on leadership roles. Yet, many people see such roles as a way to express themselves as adult, useful human beings. Assigning them to head a committee or a task force to improve productivity or the quality of work or work life may be rewarding for them.

sponse). However, they *reward* people for *exceeding* the minimum standards of the job. That's how they improve individual as well as unit productivity and help the employees stretch themselves.

Some ground rules, as shown in the sidebar, govern the effective use of rewards as reinforcers, and following them will help you distribute rewards fairly and consistently.

1. *Don't treat everyone the same way or reward everyone with the same rewards.* Everyone is different in some way, and people prefer to think of themselves as different. If you base rewards on the goals or the standards to be achieved and on individual differences, you won't fall into the trap of looking at the group rather than at the individual. This is one way you maintain or enhance people's self-esteem.

2. *Respond in a timely manner.* The people expect you to. A quick response signals interest and confidence in the other person. Failure to respond signals either that you think what the other person is doing is okay or that you don't care what he or she does. This reinforces poor performance and extinguishes good performance.

3. *Encourage autonomy.* Tell the person what he or she can do to get rewards. Then, let him or her decide whether or not to go for them—and how.

It does no harm to ask people what they want, within the known limitations of what is available, and discuss it. A perfect time and place for discussing payoffs is during some type of performance review or career planning session. Such a discussion makes it very much easier to decide what turns on another person than deciding by guessing.

4. *Take corrective action in a timely and fair manner.* Employees expect this from you also.

Jerry gave Bud a chance to change his behavior, but he didn't let it go on too long. Neither you nor the other person—nor the unit—can afford to let problems drag on.

To be fair, don't take corrective action in front of other people. In open-space environments, privacy's at a premium, but try to find a secluded place: one in which you hold confidential discussions, whether about positive things or negative ones.

5. *Praise appropriately, but avoid public praise with someone for whom that could be painful.* Consider this illustration.

A "headhunter," working for an employment agency that used monthly, quarterly, and annual meetings for rewarding its salespeople, set all the records for weekly, monthly, quarterly, and annual income for three years in a row. A very religious man, doing this kind of work only to make enough money to open a mission, he disliked the public recognition the company gave everyone. He felt on display, and, more important, thought that his being paraded that way put down everyone else and demotivated rather than motivated them. He looked for other forms of recognition.

At the same time, another employee thrived on recognition. When she did something, she rarely waited for the company to reward her. She let everyone know exactly what she did and how she did it. Her need for public approval filled the gap the other person created in the meetings' "show and tell time."

Being an Encourager

Although this young lady's overbearing ego annoyed almost everyone, she claimed a right most people have been taught always to refuse: She asserted her bragging rights.

She overdid it, to be sure, but she maintained a very positive perception of herself and her ability to succeed in a very difficult business. Her employer encouraged her bragging by encouraging everyone—including himself—to claim the same right for themselves. Remember, Positive Pygmalions begin by believing in themselves.

Encouragers take their own advice, practicing encouragement as well as preaching it. They role-model opening up their perceptions of reality, taking in new and different ways of doing things, asking themselves not only why things are done as they are but also why other things are not. They're creative, optimistic, and enthusiastic about themselves, other people, and life in general. Their attention to you in itself feels rewarding.

Deciding just how to reward each person reporting to you takes some thought and effort. Use the instrument in the Appendix ("Ways to Evaluate Motivation.") to decide how best to reinforce someone's work-related behavior. It points out (1) how a person sees him- or herself and (2) under what conditions he or she does the best work. Then you answer the questions of how best to reinforce the person's self-concept and how to ensure as realistically as you can the most favorable working conditions for each person.

Negative Consequences

A Pygmalion accentuates the positive but doesn't eliminate the negative, to paraphrase an old song. On the other hand, even when people's knowing and understanding the negative consequences for not doing a job or not doing it well helps, that knowledge doesn't sustain motivation. Promise to fire someone, and that motivator lasts only as long as the threat hangs over his or her head. You probably won't get the best from other people by managing through fear.

Still, the appropriate use of negative reinforcers, e.g., *withholding rewards* when performance doesn't meet or exceed standards, does help you motivate. Negative reinforcers extinguish unwanted behavior when you take corrective action to eliminate or replace unwanted behavior that affects the person's or the unit's productivity.

Punishment is the best known form of negative reinforcement and the easiest to apply. However, punishment poses an important management problem: What constitutes effective punishment?

Public punishment is sure to backfire on you. Threats of punishment may frighten some people, but they motivate no one. Their limited effectiveness lasts only as long as the threat lasts. So, what works?

Most successful encouragers appeal to people by calling their attention to how success satisfies their own needs (in addition to those of the organization). Failing to complete the job is itself a powerful driver, because personal pride in a job well done satisfies ego or self-fulfillment needs. That failure flies in the face of the needs for autonomy and personal power. It also threatens a person's ability to satisfy recognition and safety needs. The personal fear that a job won't get done, done on time, or done well threatens a person's self-esteem in ways your threats can't. The effective encourager helps people understand how their own efforts lead to meeting their own needs.

Effective negative reinforcement consists of denying people the rewards they expect for a job well done. Withholding rewards is usually more effective for modifying undesirable behavior than is the threat of firing or other fear tactics. You appeal to the other person by referring to the psychological contract.

A last look in on Jerry, shortly after he and Jan have begun talking, illustrates the point:

Jerry: Jan, we've been working together for six months, now. How do you feel about the way things have been going?

Jan: Pretty good. I'm glad they got rid of Jones. If they hadn't, I'd have quit. I've often wondered why I didn't. Well, that's history.

Jerry: How do you like the new job assignments?

Jan: I'm doing a whole lot of things I didn't ever think I could do. Learning how to operate the PC isn't as hard as I thought it would be. Eddie feels the same way. I think Bud's getting the knack of it, too, though it seems harder for him—but at least he's not making all that racket all the time. I guess I can say I'm doing more work and enjoying it more, too.

Jerry: Anything not going as well as you think it could or want it to?

Jan: Can't say that there is. No, everything's going so much better now than before—by comparison everything's just great. But [*Smiling broadly*], I'll bet you can come up with something."

Jerry: Well, when we set the standards for learning how to use the PC, we said that by now you'd be working a little faster, which is one of the reasons we put in the computerized system. I think we need to work on improving your output. I think you might work a little faster if you didn't have to stop and ask Eddie for advice about billing procedures. That would make you the most efficient you could be.

Jan: Well, I'm working as fast as I can.

Jerry: I don't think so, Jan. I believe you can work faster. I think you still haven't learned some important things you need to work more efficiently. Not interrupt Eddie so much, also.

48

Jan: [*Looking perplexed and concerned*] I don't think I can do it.

Jerry: [*Smiling*] But I do. I've seen you learn things quickly, and I think you can learn these things, too. You're a good worker, and you'll be an even better one once you learn these things. I think it'll be a feather in your cap to learn them—another skill. Not learning them can only hold you back—here, or anywhere else.

Jan: [*Genuinely puzzled, not knowing what to do*] I just don't know.

Jerry: What are the alternatives?

Jan: [*Sharply*] You mean transfer, like you told Bud?

Jerry: Jan, that's always a possibility, not a threat. We need certain things here. New ways of doing things. You're someone I've come to value, and I want you to give it a try.

[*Although intimated by math and anxious about failing, Jan feels a need to respond to Jerry's confidence.*]

Jan: You think I can do it?

Jerry: Yes.

Jan: You're probably right. I *can* do it, but, that means learning some math. I've never been good at it.

Jerry: The computer and I will help. There's some software I can get that'll teach you the math, and I can teach you the billing procedures.

Jan: I hear you. When do we start?

Jerry: I'll have the software in here by week's end.

What Did Jerry Do?

Review the dialogue with Jan, the way you did before, to see the eleven ways Jerry encouraged Jan to stretch. When you're finished, check your answers against the list in Exhibit 5. Then, continue reading.

Exhibit 5. More of Jerry's encouragers with Jan.

1. He gave Jan a chance to talk about her work and possibly identify some of her own shortcomings.
2. He nonjudgmentally detailed the problem, giving immediate, specific, and accurate feedback.
3. He was honest with her.
4. He let Jan know that he had confidence in her ability to do good work and to solve this problem.
5. He mentioned both positive and negative consequences.
6. He let Jan choose whether or not to do something about the situation.
7. He took responsibility for *helping* to solve the problem.
8. He reassured Jan that he would help.
9. He expressed his confidence in her abilities.
10. He gave credit for good work.
11. He listened, giving undivided attention, at all times.

Conclusion

You *can* motivate. Getting the best from other people means creating a productive environment and becoming an encourager—a Positive Pygmalion. But, don't demand too much of yourself.

As Maslow said, *motivation* comes from within the person—from his or her drivers. No matter how hard you work, if the other person's desire or skills aren't there, you can't do anything with reinforcers or incentives you supply from the outside.

You can motivate other people as long as you expect to get the best. You can set high but realistic standards and expect people, including yourself, to meet them. If you're enthusiastic about the group's goals and mission, about the people in the group, and about yourself, people will usually respond in kind.

At the same time, you have to allow people to make mistakes from which they can learn. They must have the autonomy to work on their own shortcomings and improve their productivity. While recognizing people for what they do and rewarding them for their successes or accomplishments, you need to give them negative feedback or they won't know what you think or feel. They might not know that they're not meeting the standards.

Understand what people want for themselves and what they're willing to give in order to get what they want or need. That way you know which rewards (or their denial) will work for them and which will not. Your decisions will be more appropriate, and theirs will meet the needs of the situation.

Encourage cooperation within the group and reasonable competitiveness with other groups. You want the people who have to work together every day to work as a team, to support one another's efforts, and to help and encourage each other. Have them competing with themselves against standards, and if they must compete against other people, let them compete—in a friendly way—with other units.

As in any situation where people work together, your employees will disagree with each other. You want to encourage productive disagreement; it's the stuff of which creativity and innovation are made. At the same time, you want to help resolve conflicts that could tear at the fabric of the unit's teamwork.

Your employees want you to meet these expectations. It's part of their psychological contract with you that by being the very best you can be, you'll encourage them to be their very best as well.

Appendix
Ways to Evaluate Motivation

Introduction

No one has designed a foolproof method for evaluating what encourages people to do their best. You could ask each person under your supervision to complete a copy of "What Drives Me?" and discuss the results with them. That would profit everyone. Or, you can use the following guide to fairly estimate what you think you need to do to provide the proper incentives for each person.

Of course, you can't always supply exactly the reward the other person wants. Then you have to be creative and hit on one you can provide that would come as close to the employee's payoffs as you can get. Working on this together could make your job a lot easier.

Instructions

In Part I: Self-Concept, consider how the employee sees him- or herself. Then, think of what you can offer as an incentive to help that person stay motivated. Whatever you offer, it has to match with how the individual sees him- or herself or it won't work.

In Part II: Working Conditions, consider the conditions under which the employee produces the most and the best work. Not every one of the items on the list will fit for any one employee. Some are mutually

---

Adapted from Donald H. Weiss, *How to Delegate Effectively*, a Cassette/Workbook program (New York: AMACOM, 1987).

exclusive. Decide what you can allow or provide and what you can't in order to help the person work under the best conditions possible for him or her.

Use a separate copy of the form for each person reporting to you. Use the first two lines to model your own work, and since the list is not exhaustive, add anything you think is relevant to the person whose behavior you're evaluating.

Name: _____

Behavior	Ways to Encourage the Behavior

Part 1: Self-Concept
How does _____ see him-/herself?

- As a self-starter

  Let him/her set his/her deadlines.

  _____

  _____

- As a hard worker

  Praise his/her punctuality.

  _____

  _____

  _____

Part 2: Working Conditions
What does _____ prefer?

- To receive detailed instructions and carry them out faithfully

  _____

  _____

  _____

- To work things out by him-/herself

  _____

  _____

  _____

- To work slowly and give a lot of attention to detail and logical thinking

  _____

  _____

- To work at a fast pace, making quick but intelligent decisions

  _____

  _____

  _____

- To take responsibility for other people (lead)

  _____

  _____

  _____

- To work autonomously, but gets along well with others

  _____

  _____

  _____

- To work in a team, with close work and social relations

  _____

  _____

  _____

- Very little recognition or
  attention from others

  _____

  _____

  _____

- A lot of recognition and
  attention from others

  _____

  _____

  _____

- To express his/her feelings easily and con-
  structively

  _____

  _____

  _____

- To receive feedback
  whether positive or
  negative (as opposed
  to receiving none at all)

  _____

  _____

  _____

Index

About the Author

Donald H. Weiss, Ph.D., of Millers' Mutual Insurance in Alton, Illinois, has been engaged in education and training for over 26 years and has written numerous articles, books, audio cassette/workbook programs, and video training films on effective sales and supervisory or management skills. He speaks regularly on stress management and other personal development subjects, and has produced a variety of related printed or recorded materials.

During his career, Dr. Weiss has been the Manager of Special Projects for a training and development firm, the Manager of Management Training for an insurance company, the Director of Training for an employment agency group, a training consultant, and a writer-producer-director of video training tapes. He also has taught at several universities and colleges in Texas, including the University of Texas at Arlington and Texas Christian University, in Forth Worth.

Currently, Dr. Weiss is Corporate Training Director for Millers' Mutual Insurance.